Contents

21st Century – page 2
Transfers I – page 6
First Goals I – page 9
Red Cards – page 11
Memorable Goals – page 14
Memorable Games – page 17
Transfers II – page 20
Cup Games – page 23
First Goals II – page 26

21st Century answers – page 29
Transfers I answers – page 34
First Goals I answers – page 38
Red Cards answers – page 40
Memorable Goals answers – page 44
Memorable Games answers – page 47
Transfers II answers – page 51
Cup Games answers – page 55
First Goals II answers – page 59

21st Century

1) Who was manager of West Ham at the beginning of the 21st Century?

2) Who scored the first goal for West Ham in the 21st Century, during a 2-2 draw with Newcastle United?

3) What shirt number has Michail Antonio worn since he joined West Ham?

4) Who made his debut aged just 16 years and 7 months old in a 2-0 away win against Arsenal in August 2015?

5) Who took over from Gianfranco Zola as manager in 2010?

6) West Ham were relegated from the Premier League in 2003 despite winning how many points?

7) Who became the first Algerian to represent the club after signing in 2016?

8) West Ham played with no shirt sponsor against West Brom in 2008 after which company collapsed?

9) What was the score in Alan Curbishley's first game as West Ham manager in December 2006?

10) Mark Noble made his West Ham first-team debut against which side in the League Cup in August 2004?

11) Teddy Sheringham holds the record as the oldest ever Premier League goal scorer after he netted at the age of 40 years, 8 months and 24 days against which team in December 2006?

12) Kevin Nolan took over the club captaincy from which player in 2011?

13) Which Slovenian team did West Ham beat 3-0 in the first competitive game at the Olympic Stadium?

14) Andy Carroll scored a 94th minute winner to secure a 2-1 victory over West Brom in January 2018, but which former West Ham manager was in charge of the opposition?

15) In what year did David Sullivan and David Gold take over the ownership of the club?

16) West Ham prevent Tottenham from qualifying for the Champions League on the last day of the 2005/06 season by beating them by what score?

17) Who scored a calamitous own goal in the defeat to Burnley in November 2019?

18) Who scored a hat-trick for the Hammers in the 3-3 draw with Arsenal in April 2016?

19) What was the result in Slaven Bilic's last game in charge?

20) Who was West Ham's top scorer in the 2005/06 season with 14 goals?

21) The October 2014 home match with Manchester City was almost delayed after smoke appeared from what unusual object?

Transfers I

1) Which striker was brought in from Lyon in May 2000?

2) West Ham signed which two players from Arsenal in June 2000?

3) Defender Christian Dailly was bought from which team in January 2001?

4) Who was sold to Chelsea in June 2001?

5) Tomas Repka arrived in September 2001 from which Italian club?

6) Which experience striker came in from Tottenham Hotspur in January 2003?

7) Goalkeeper Shaka Hislop left in July 2002 to sign for which team?

8) Midfielder Rob Lee arrived on a free transfer from where in August 2003?

9) From which club was Nigel Reo-Coker bought in January 2004?

10) Who was Trevor Sinclair sold to in July 2003?

11) Paulo Di Canio left on a free to sign for which team in August 2003?

12) Which winger was signed on a free from Manchester United in August 2004?

13) West Ham sold which central midfield player to Tottenham in August 2004?

14) Which centre forward arrived at the club from Norwich City in January 2006?

15) Who did Steve Lomas sign for after leaving the club in August 2005?

16) From which club did Javier Mascherano and Carlos Tevez arrive in the summer of 2006?

17) Teddy Sheringham left West Ham in July 2007 before signing for which team?

18) West Ham signed which two midfielders from Newcastle United in August 2007?

19) To which team was Yossi Benayoun sold in the summer of 2007?

20) Which striker was signed on a free transfer from Livorno in October 2008?

21) Two defenders were sold to Sunderland in the summer on 2008, who were they?

22) Which club did Craig Bellamy join from West Ham in January 2009?

23) Who did Lee Bowyer sign for after leaving the club in July 2009?

First Goals I – Name the clubs that these players scored their first goal for the club against

1) Mark Noble

2) Dean Ashton

3) Sebastian Haller

4) Jermain Defoe

5) Felipe Anderson

6) Matty Taylor

7) Freddie Sears

8) Declan Rice

9) Bobby Zamora

10) Craig Bellamy

11) Carlton Cole

12) Matthew Etherington

13) Teddy Sheringham

14) Freddie Kanoute

Red Cards

1) West Ham conceded a late equaliser to draw 1-1 with Leicester in October 2018 after which player had been sent off?

2) Which player was sent off inside 15 minutes as West Ham went down to a 3-1 defeat away to Arsenal in January 2003?

3) Who scored but was then later dismissed in the 3-0 win against Liverpool at Anfield in August 2015?

4) Who was sent off for dissent in the last minute of the draw at home to Fulham in December 2002?

5) Who received a red card for kicking out at an opponent during the 2-1 loss away to Fulham in January 2014?

6) Which centre back was dismissed late on in the 2-0 defeat at Watford in October 2015?

7) West Ham lost 3-2 in the last minute against Southampton in August 2017 having twice come from behind to equalise after which player was sent off for elbowing Jack Stephens?

8) Which player was sent off for receiving two yellow cards in stoppage time during the 3-2 defeat away to Spurs in November 2016?

9) James Tomkins was sent off in a 3-1 loss away to which team in May 2009?

10) Goalkeeper Adrian was sent off for a dangerous, studs up challenge on which Leicester City player in August 2015?

11) Andy Carroll was controversially sent off after tangling with which Swansea City player in the 2-0 home win in February 2014?

12) Against which side was Stuart Pearce dismissed for two bookable offences in March 2001?

13) Who was suspended for the 2006 FA Cup Final after being sent off in a League match against Liverpool for clashing with Luis Garcia?

14) Which midfielder was shown a red card late on during the 1-1 draw with Birmingham City in February 2008?

15) Who was shown two yellow cards in the 0-0 draw at Aston Villa in September 2019?

Memorable Goals

1) Paulo Di Canio scored his incredible volley versus Wimbledon in March 2000 past which goalkeeper?

2) In September 2002 Di Canio won the Premier League Goal of the Month when he flicked the ball up before volleying in with his left foot from long-range against which side?

3) Carlton Cole rounded off a sweeping team move by curling a first-time finish into the far corner against who in March 2009?

4) Which player scored with a solo run and deft finish to round off the 3-0 win away at Tottenham in October 2013?

5) Dimitri Payet hit a fantastic free kick which dipped dramatically into the far corner against which side in April 2016?

6) Bobby Zamora squeezed his shot in between the keepers legs after a brilliant solo run against who in December 2005?

7) Who smashed in a volley on the turn from the edge of the box to open the scoring in the 2-1 win versus Fulham in January 2006?

8) In the same game who scored the second by twisting and turning on the edge of the box before producing a sublime chip?

9) Who scored with a powerful overhead kick in the 3-0 win over Crystal Palace in January 2017?

10) Trevor Sinclair scored a sensational scissor kick in December 2000 against which team?

11) Andy Carroll won the Goal of the Month competition for March 2013 when he let the ball drop over his shoulder before hitting a controlled volley with his right foot against which team?

12) Who rifled a scorching shot into the top corner against Tottenham at Wembley in January 2018?

Memorable Games

1) Winston Reid headed the last ever goal at Upton Park as West Ham dramatically beat Manchester United by what score in May 2016?

2) West Ham secured their Premier League survival on the last day of the 2006/07 season when which player scored the only goal in a 1-0 win over Manchester United at Old Trafford?

3) West Ham won a Premier League classic when they beat Bradford City 5-4 in February 2000, which young goalkeeper came on as a substitute for West Ham to make his debut?

4) Who scored the winner as West Ham beat Blackpool 2-1 in the 2012 Championship Play Off Final?

5) West Ham inflicted Tottenham's first defeat at their new stadium when which player scored the only goal in a 1-0 win in April 2019?

6) West Ham won 2-1 away at Wigan in March 2006 when who scored the winner in the last minute?

7) Who scored the only goal as Crystal Palace beat West Ham 1-0 in the Championship Play Off Final in 2004?

8) The next season West Ham bounced back to beat which team 1-0 in the 2005 Play Off Final through a goal from Bobby Zamora?

9) Who scored a hat-trick as the Hammers beat Brighton 6-0 in the Championship in April 2012?

10) Which team did West Ham beat 4-3 in the Championship in September 2011?

11) Which team beat West Ham 7-1 in the Premier League in October 2001?

12) Who scored the only goal of the game deep into second half injury time to beat Sunderland 1-0 in October 2016?

13) What was the final score as West Ham beat Manchester United in September 2018?

14) West Ham sealed Premier League survival by beating Tottenham Hotspur 2-0 in May 2014, which Spurs player scored an own goal to open the scoring?

15) Who scored the only goal at Stamford Bridge as Chelsea were beaten 1-0 in November 2019?

Transfers II

1) Which striker arrived from Blackburn Rovers in February 2010?

2) From which German club was forward Demba Ba signed in January 2011?

3) Which midfielder was bought from Newcastle United in June 2011?

4) Ricardo Vaz Te arrived from where in January 2012?

5) Which goalkeeper was brought in from Bolton in June 2012?

6) Joe Cole signed on a free transfer from which club in January 2013?

7) Who did Rob Green sign for after leaving West Ham in June 2012?

8) Which forward arrived from Velez Sarsfield in May 2014?

9) From which club was Aaron Cresswell signed in July 2014?

10) Who did Joe Cole sign for after leaving the club in June 2014?

11) From which French club did West Ham buy Dimitri Payet in June 2015?

12) Which player did West Ham buy from Juventus in July 2015?

13) Who did West Ham sell to Middlesbrough in July 2015?

14) From which club was Andre Ayew purchased in August 2016?

15) Which right back was signed on a free transfer from Manchester City in the summer of 2017?

16) From which German club did Javier Hernandez arrive in July 2017?

17) Which defender arrived on a free transfer from Marseille in February 2018?

18) Who left West Ham to sign for Chinese Club Dalian Yifang in February 2018?

19) From where did Andriy Yarmolenko arrive in the summer of 2018?

20) Who was sold to Crystal Palace in August 2018?

21) Which goalkeeper was signed on a free from Millwall in June 2019?

22) From where was Sebastian Haller bought in July 2019?

23) Jarrod Bowen was purchased in the January transfer window of 2020 from which team?

Cup Games

1) Paulo Di Canio scored the winner in the FA Cup Fourth Round tie at Old Trafford in 2001 when which Manchester United goalkeeper stood stationary appealing for offside as Di Canio broke through on goal?

2) Which team knocked West Ham out in the Qualifying Round of the Europa League in both 2015 and 2016?

3) Who scored the only goal as West Ham beat Middlesbrough in the FA Cup Semi Final of 2006?

4) West Ham were beaten 4-2 by which lower league side in the FA Cup Fourth Round in 2019?

5) By what score did Manchester United beat West Ham in the 2003 FA Cup Fourth Round?

6) Which three West Ham players missed in the penalty shoot-out as Liverpool came from behind to lift the FA Cup in 2006?

7) Robin Van Persie scored a late equaliser to make it 2-2 and force a replay in the FA Cup Third Round in 2013, but who had scored both goals for West Ham

8) Which Italian side beat West Ham 4-0 on aggregate in the UEFA Cup First Round in 2006?

9) Against which team did West Ham win 5-1 away in the FA Cup Fifth Round in 2016?

10) Manchester City humiliated West Ham in the League Cup Semi Final of 2014 by beating them by what aggregate score line?

11) Birmingham City knocked West Ham out of the League Cup at the Semi Final stage in 2011 after which player scored the winning goal in extra time?

12) Which former Manchester United player scored a brace in the 4-0 win in the League Cup Fifth Round in November 2010?

13) What was the score as West Ham demolished Macclesfield in the League Cup Third Round in September 2018?

14) Who scored the winning penalty in the shoot-out as the Hammers knocked Everton out of the FA Cup in 2015?

First Goals II

1) Kevin Nolan

2) James Collins

3) Paul Konchesky

4) Jack Collison

5) Lee Bowyer

6) Marlon Harewood

7) Scott Parker

8) Cheikhou Kouyate

9) Dimitri Payet

10) Andy Carroll

11) Aaron Cresswell

12) Marko Arnautovic

13) Robert Snodgrass

14) Michail Antonio

Answers

21st Century – Answers

1) Who was manager of West Ham at the beginning of the 21st Century?
Harry Redknapp

2) Who scored the first goal for West Ham in the 21st Century, during a 2-2 draw with Newcastle United?
Frank Lampard

3) What shirt number has Michail Antonio worn since he joined West Ham?
30

4) Who made his debut aged just 16 years and 7 months old in a 2-0 away win against Arsenal in August 2015?
Reece Oxford

5) Who took over from Gianfranco Zola as manager in 2010?
Avram Grant

6) West Ham were relegated from the Premier League in 2003 despite winning how many points?
42

7) Who became the first Algerian to represent the club after signing in 2016?
Sofiane Feghouli

8) West Ham played with no shirt sponsor against West Brom in 2008 after which company collapsed?
XL

9) What was the score in Alan Curbishley's first game as West Ham manager in December 2006?
West Ham 1-0 Manchester United

10) Mark Noble made his West Ham first-team debut against which side in the League Cup in August 2004?
Southend United

11) Teddy Sheringham holds the record as the oldest ever Premier League goal scorer after he netted at the age of 40 years, 8 months and 24 days against which team in December 2006?
Portsmouth

12) Kevin Nolan took over the club captaincy from which player in 2011?
Matthew Upson

13) Which Slovenian team did West Ham beat 3-0 in the first competitive game at the Olympic Stadium?
NK Domzale

14) Andy Carroll scored a 94th minute winner to secure a 2-1 victory over West Brom in January 2018, but which former West Ham manager was in charge of the opposition?
Alan Pardew

15) In what year did David Sullivan and David Gold take over the ownership of the club?
2010

16) West Ham prevent Tottenham from qualifying for the Champions League on the last day of the 2005/06 season by beating them by what score?
2-1

17) Who scored a calamitous own goal in the defeat to Burnley in November 2019?
Roberto

18) Who scored a hat-trick for the Hammers in the 3-3 draw with Arsenal in April 2016?
Andy Carroll

19) What was the result in Slaven Bilic's last game in charge?
West Ham 1-4 Liverpool

20) Who was West Ham's top scorer in the 2005/06 season with 14 goals?
Marlon Harewood

21) The October 2014 home match with Manchester City was almost delayed after smoke appeared from what unusual object?
The bubble machine

Transfers I – Answers

1) Which striker was brought in from Lyon in May 2000?
   Freddie Kanoute

2) West Ham signed which two players from Arsenal in June 2000?
   Nigel Winterburn and Davor Suker

3) Defender Christian Dailly was bought from which team in January 2001?
   Blackburn Rovers

4) Who was sold to Chelsea in June 2001?
   Frank Lampard

5) Tomas Repka arrived in September 2001 from which Italian club?
   Fiorentina

6) Which experience striker came in from Tottenham Hotspur in January 2003?
   Les Ferdinand

7) Goalkeeper Shaka Hislop left in July 2002 to sign for which team?
Portsmouth

8) Midfielder Rob Lee arrived on a free transfer from where in August 2003?
Derby County

9) From which club was Nigel Reo-Coker bought in January 2004?
Wimbledon

10) Who was Trevor Sinclair sold to in July 2003?
Manchester City

11) Paulo Di Canio left on a free to sign for which team in August 2003?
Charlton Athletic

12) Which winger was signed on a free from Manchester United in August 2004?
Luke Chadwick

13) West Ham sold which central midfield player to Tottenham in August 2004?
Michael Carrick

14) Which centre forward arrived at the club from Norwich City in January 2006?
Dean Ashton

15) Who did Steve Lomas sign for after leaving the club in August 2005?
QPR

16) From which club did Javier Mascherano and Carlos Tevez arrive in the summer of 2006?
Corinthians

17) Teddy Sheringham left West Ham in July 2007 before signing for which team?
Colchester United

18) West Ham signed which two midfielders from Newcastle United in August 2007?
Kieron Dyer and Nolberto Solano

19) To which team was Yossi Benayoun sold in the summer of 2007?
Liverpool

20) Which striker was signed on a free transfer from Livorno in October 2008?
Diego Tristan

21) Two defenders were sold to Sunderland in the summer on 2008, who were they?
Anton Ferdinand and George McCartney

22) Which club did Craig Bellamy join from West Ham in January 2009?
Manchester City

23) Who did Lee Bowyer sign for after leaving the club in July 2009?
Birmingham City

First Goals I – Answers

1) Mark Noble
   Brighton

2) Dean Ashton
   Sunderland

3) Sebastian Haller
   Watford

4) Jermain Defoe
   Ipswich Town

5) Felipe Anderson
   Manchester United

6) Matty Taylor
   Portsmouth

7) Freddie Sears
   Blackburn Rovers

8) Declan Rice
   Arsenal

9) Bobby Zamora
   Bradford City

10) Craig Bellamy
    Bristol Rovers

11) Carlton Cole
    Charlton Athletic

12) Matthew Etherington
    Crewe Alexandra

13) Teddy Sheringham
    Reading

14) Freddie Kanoute
    Wimbledon

Red Cards – Answers

1) West Ham conceded a late equaliser to draw 1-1 with Leicester in October 2018 after which player had been sent off?
Mark Noble

2) Which player was sent off inside 15 minutes as West Ham went down to a 3-1 defeat away to Arsenal in January 2003?
Steve Lomas

3) Who scored but was then later dismissed in the 3-0 win against Liverpool at Anfield in August 2015?
Mark Noble

4) Who was sent off for dissent in the last minute of the draw at home to Fulham in December 2002?
Tomas Repka

5) Who received a red card for kicking out at an opponent during the 2-1 loss away to Fulham in January 2014?
Kevin Nolan

6) Which centre back was dismissed late on in the 2-0 defeat at Watford in October 2015?
James Collins

7) West Ham lost 3-2 in the last minute against Southampton in August 2017 having twice come from behind to equalise after which player was sent off for elbowing Jack Stephens?
Marko Arnautovic

8) Which player was sent off for receiving two yellow cards in stoppage time during the 3-2 defeat away to Spurs in November 2016?
Winston Reid

9) James Tomkins was sent off in a 3-1 loss away to which team in May 2009?
Everton

10) Goalkeeper Adrian was sent off for a dangerous, studs up challenge on which Leicester City player in August 2015?
Jamie Vardy

11) Andy Carroll was controversially sent off after tangling with which Swansea City player in the 2-0 home win in February 2014?
Chico Flores

12) Against which side was Stuart Pearce dismissed for two bookable offences in March 2001?
Everton

13) Who was suspended for the 2006 FA Cup Final after being sent off in a League match against Liverpool for clashing with Luis Garcia?
Hayden Mullins

14) Which midfielder was shown a red card late on during the 1-1 draw with Birmingham City in February 2008?
Lee Bowyer

15) Who was shown two yellow cards in the 0-0 draw at Aston Villa in September 2019?
Arthur Masuaku

Memorable Goals – Answers

1) Paulo Di Canio scored his incredible volley versus Wimbledon in March 2000 past which goalkeeper?
   Neil Sullivan

2) In September 2002 Di Canio won the Premier League Goal of the Month when he flicked the ball up before volleying in with his left foot from long-range against which side?
   Chelsea

3) Carlton Cole rounded off a sweeping team move by curling a first-time finish into the far corner against who in March 2009?
   Wigan Athletic

4) Which player scored with a solo run and deft finish to round off the 3-0 win away at Tottenham in October 2013?
   Ravel Morrison

5) Dimitri Payet hit a fantastic free kick which dipped dramatically into the far corner against which side in April 2016?
Crystal Palace

6) Bobby Zamora squeezed his shot in between the keepers legs after a brilliant solo run against who in December 2005?
Birmingham City

7) Who smashed in a volley on the turn from the edge of the box to open the scoring in the 2-1 win versus Fulham in January 2006?
Anton Ferdinand

8) In the same game who scored the second by twisting and turning on the edge of the box before producing a sublime chip?
Yossi Benayoun

9) Who scored with a powerful overhead kick in the 3-0 win over Crystal Palace in January 2017?
Andy Carroll

10) Trevor Sinclair scored a sensational scissor kick in December 2000 against which team?
Derby County

11) Andy Carroll won the Goal of the Month competition for March 2013 when he let the ball drop over his shoulder before hitting a controlled volley with his right foot against which team?
West Brom

12) Who rifled a scorching shot into the top corner against Tottenham at Wembley in January 2018?
Pedro Obiang

Memorable Games – Answers

1) Winston Reid headed the last ever goal at Upton Park as West Ham dramatically beat Manchester United by what score in May 2016?
   3-2

2) West Ham secured their Premier League survival on the last day of the 2006/07 season when which player scored the only goal in a 1-0 win over Manchester United at Old Trafford?
   Carlos Tevez

3) West Ham won a Premier League classic when they beat Bradford City 5-4 in February 2000, which young goalkeeper came on as a substitute for West Ham to make his debut?
   Stephen Bywater

4) Who scored the winner as West Ham beat Blackpool 2-1 in the 2012 Championship Play Off Final?
   Ricardo Vaz Te

5) West Ham inflicted Tottenham's first defeat at their new stadium when which player scored the only goal in a 1-0 win in April 2019?
Michail Antonio

6) West Ham won 2-1 away at Wigan in March 2006 when who scored the winner in the last minute?
Nigel Reo-Coker

7) Who scored the only goal as Crystal Palace beat West Ham 1-0 in the Championship Play Off Final in 2004?
Neil Shipperley

8) The next season West Ham bounced back to beat which team 1-0 in the 2005 Play Off Final through a goal from Bobby Zamora?
Preston North End

9) Who scored a hat-trick as the Hammers beat Brighton 6-0 in the Championship in April 2012?
Ricardo Vaz Te

10) Which team did West Ham beat 4-3 in the Championship in September 2011?
Portsmouth

11) Which team beat West Ham 7-1 in the Premier League in October 2001?
Blackburn Rovers

12) Who scored the only goal of the game deep into second half injury time to beat Sunderland 1-0 in October 2016?
Winston Reid

13) What was the final score as West Ham beat Manchester United in September 2018?
3-1

14) West Ham sealed Premier League survival by beating Tottenham Hotspur 2-0 in May 2014, which Spurs player scored an own goal to open the scoring?
Harry Kane

15) Who scored the only goal at Stamford Bridge as Chelsea were beaten 1-0 in November 2019?
Aaron Cresswell

Transfers II – Answers

1) Which striker arrived from Blackburn Rovers in February 2010?
Benni McCarthy

2) From which German club was forward Demba Ba signed in January 2011?
Hoffenheim

3) Which midfielder was bought from Newcastle United in June 2011?
Kevin Nolan

4) Ricardo Vaz Te arrived from where in January 2012?
Barnsley

5) Which goalkeeper was brought in from Bolton in June 2012?
Jussi Jaaskelainen

6) Joe Cole signed on a free transfer from which club in January 2013?
Liverpool

7) Who did Rob Green sign for after leaving West Ham in June 2012?
QPR

8) Which forward arrived from Velez Sarsfield in May 2014?
Mauro Zarate

9) From which club was Aaron Cresswell signed in July 2014?
Ipswich Town

10) Who did Joe Cole sign for after leaving the club in June 2014?
Aston Villa

11) From which French club did West Ham buy Dimitri Payet in June 2015?
Marseille

12) Which player did West Ham buy from Juventus in July 2015?
Angelo Ogbonna

13) Who did West Ham sell to Middlesbrough in July 2015?
Stewart Downing

14) From which club was Andre Ayew purchased in August 2016?
Swansea City

15) Which right back was signed on a free transfer from Manchester City in the summer of 2017?
Pablo Zabaleta

16) From which German club did Javier Hernandez arrive in July 2017?
Bayer Leverkusen

17) Which defender arrived on a free transfer from Marseille in February 2018?
Patrice Evra

18) Who left West Ham to sign for Chinese Club Dalian Yifang in February 2018?
Jose Fonte

19) From where did Andriy Yarmolenko arrive in the summer of 2018?
Borussia Dortmund

20) Who was sold to Crystal Palace in August 2018?
Cheikhou Kouyate

21) Which goalkeeper was signed on a free from Millwall in June 2019?
David Martin

22) From where was Sebastian Haller bought in July 2019?
Eintracht Frankfurt

23) Jarrod Bowen was purchased in the January transfer window of 2020 from which team?
Hull City

Cup Games – Answers

1) Paulo Di Canio scored the winner in the FA Cup Fourth Round tie at Old Trafford in 2001 when which Manchester United goalkeeper stood stationary appealing for offside as Di Canio broke through on goal?
Fabian Barthez

2) Which team knocked West Ham out in the Qualifying Round of the Europa League in both 2015 and 2016?
Astra Giurgiu

3) Who scored the only goal as West Ham beat Middlesbrough in the FA Cup Semi Final of 2006?
Marlon Harewood

4) West Ham were beaten 4-2 by which lower league side in the FA Cup Fourth Round in 2019?
AFC Wimbledon

5) By what score did Manchester United beat West Ham in the 2003 FA Cup Fourth Round?
6-0

6) Which three West Ham players missed in the penalty shoot-out as Liverpool came from behind to lift the FA Cup in 2006?
Bobby Zamora, Paul Konchesky and Anton Ferdinand

7) Robin Van Persie scored a late equaliser to make it 2-2 and force a replay in the FA Cup Third Round in 2013, but who had scored both goals for West Ham
James Collins

8) Which Italian side beat West Ham 4-0 on aggregate in the UEFA Cup First Round in 2006?
Palermo

9) Against which team did West Ham win 5-1 away in the FA Cup Fifth Round in 2016?
Blackburn Rovers

10) Manchester City humiliated West Ham in the League Cup Semi Final of 2014 by beating them by what aggregate score line?
9-0

11) Birmingham City knocked West Ham out of the League Cup at the Semi Final stage in 2011 after which player scored the winning goal in extra time?
Craig Gardner

12) Which former Manchester United player scored a brace in the 4-0 win in the League Cup Fifth Round in November 2010?
Jonathan Spector

13) What was the score as West Ham demolished Macclesfield in the League Cup Third Round in September 2018?
8-0

14) Who scored the winning penalty in the shoot-out as the Hammers knocked Everton out of the FA Cup in 2015?
Adrian

First Goals II – Answers

1) Kevin Nolan
   Doncaster Rovers

2) James Collins
   Portsmouth

3) Paul Konchesky
   Sunderland

4) Jack Collison
   Everton

5) Lee Bowyer
   Wigan Athletic

6) Marlon Harewood
   Wigan Athletic

7) Scott Parker
   Middlesbrough

8) Cheikhou Kouyate
   Arsenal

9) Dimitri Payet
   Leicester City

10) Andy Carroll
    Tottenham Hotspur

11) Aaron Cresswell
    Newcastle United

12) Marko Arnautovic
    Chelsea

13) Robert Snodgrass
    Macclesfield Town

14) Michail Antonio
    Southampton

Printed in Great Britain
by Amazon